Road Trip
An Integrated Unit of Study

by

Marian Diana Costello
Carol Rito McGrath
Dagmar Kosack Rutzen

© 1993

ECS
Learning Systems
INC.

Printed in the U.S.A.

Editors: **Lori Mammen and Jennifer Knoblock**
Page Layout & Graphics: **Kathryn Riches**
Cover/Book Design: **Educational Media Services**

Other titles in the Primary Thematic Unit Series (Grades K-4):

ECS9757	Animals
ECS9781	Bears Everywhere
ECS979X	Dinosaurs
ECS9730	Fall Harvest
ECS9803	Fairy Tales
ECS9811	Folktales
ECS9889	Love and Friendship
ECS9765	Maps and Globes
ECS9749	Native Americans
ECS982X	Oceans
ECS9838	Plants
ECS9846	Sports
ECS9854	Stars and Planets
ECS9862	Toys
ECS9870	Ugh! Bugs!
ECS9773	Weather

ECS9072	Writing Warm-Ups™	(Grades K-6)
ECS9455	Writing Warm-Ups™ Two	(Grades K-6)
ECS9471	Quick Thinking™	(Grades K-6)
ECS9617	Booklinks	(Grades 3-8)
ECS951X	Building Language Power, I	(Grades 4-9)
ECS9528	Building Language Power, II	(Grades 4-9)
ECS9684	Building Language Power, III	(Grades 4-9)
ECS9625	Passageways	(Grades 5-9)

To order, contact your local school supply store, or write/call:

**ECS Learning Systems, Inc.
P.O. Box 791437
San Antonio, Texas 78279-1437
1-800-68-TEACH**

ISBN 0-944459-71-4

Table of Contents

Introduction

Have you ever felt as though you were being bombarded with more and more subject matter to be covered in the classroom and not enough time? Not only are teachers expected to teach the basics, but today they are expected to include such topics as career education, consumer education, drug awareness, and computer literacy. This unit keeps busy teachers, as well as the unique needs of their students, in mind.

One way to help teachers cover the increasingly vast amount of material in the same amount of classroom time is through the interdisciplinary approach (I.A.). The I.A. is a way to integrate subjects from the curriculum so that they overlap and are blended together. Instead of being taught in isolation, the I.A. shows the relationship between subjects. It provides high interest, skills based activities and is more child centered than teacher centered. It emphasizes process, not product. All of this makes student learning more relevant.

The unit, *Road Trip*, is one solution to the problem of the crowded curriculum. In this unit teachers integrate only those areas that "fit" their curriculum objectives. This allows teachers to meet the needs of the students and fulfill the required mandates of the state.

The I.A. helps teachers cover objectives from many areas within one unit of study. Its purpose is to provide students with real-life applications of lessons learned in the classroom. This unit incorporates mathematics, social studies, language arts, health, and fine arts.

During this unit the students will be taking an imaginary 14-day trip. In order to complete this trip, they will be given certain parameters. The destination you select should enable students to "visit" many places of historical significance.

 ©1993 ECS LEARNING SYSTEMS, INC., SAN ANTONIO, TEXAS

More opportunities are offered to students to discover and experience the world around them. For example, they will use math skills to calculate mileage as well as meal, lodging, and fuel costs. Map skills will be used to trace travel routes. Response journals will allow students to record their thoughts and feelings. The I.A. gives students a purpose for using the skills they have learned in the classroom by applying them to real-life situations. The I.A. offers many student benefits, such as the following:

Having fun while learning

Meeting new challenges

Planning cooperatively

Thinking critically

Becoming self-reliant

Maintaining a high interest level

Using creative problem solving skills

Participating in small/large group interaction

Brainstorming new ideas

Enhancing motivation

Having freedom of choice

©1993 ECS LEARNING SYSTEMS, INC., SAN ANTONIO, TEXAS

Overview

Unit Goals

To transfer what is learned in math class to real-life situations

To use good listening skills

To practice the social skills necessary to be an effective group member

To tie in historical events to the places where they happened

To share what is learned with others

To use good public speaking skills

To use reading and writing for a purpose

To use research skills

To develop the ability to interpret data

To involve parents in the learning process

©1993 ECS LEARNING SYSTEMS, INC., SAN ANTONIO, TEXAS

The student will be able to:

OBJECTIVES	SUBJECT(S)	ACTIVITIES

Make estimations
Add, subtract, multiply, and divide whole numbers
	Social studies
	Math
		Estimate and record:
		  - How much will be spent on food, lodging, and gas for the trip
		  - Distance to the destination
		  - How many times they will need to stop for gas

Use map and globe skills	Social studies Math Reading	Use a map key Use distance scales to figure out mileage Make a mileage chart Plot a route on a road map
Use research skills	Language arts Social studies	Use the card catalog Organize information Take notes

Write business letters	Language arts	Write to:
		  -Chambers of commerce
		  -State travel/tourist information bureaus
		  -Major hotel/motel chains
		  -Campgrounds
		  -Major restaurant chains for menus

Plan healthy meals within a budget	Health Math Writing	Complete "Food Budget" sheet

OBJECTIVES	SUBJECT(S)	ACTIVITIES
Keep a daily expense log	Math Writing Reading	Create and complete the log
Measure distance on a map Figure out miles per gallon and cost of fuel Round money to nearest cent Use ratios	Math	Complete "Fuel Sheet"

Prepare for trip
Find averages
Present information orally
	Reading
	Writing
	Math
	Social studies
	Language arts
		Fill out "Places to Visit" sheet
		Fill out "All About My Trip"
		  sheet
		Give a presentation (See "Oral
		  Presentation" sheet)

Develop vocabulary skills	Reading Social studies Speech	Complete "Vocabulary Knowledge Rating" sheet
Use graphing skills	Math	Make a graph for either daily mileage or daily expenses
Develop interview skills	Speech Writing	Talk to parents about trip tips and record responses
Keep a response journal	Reading Writing Social studies	Write entries in travel journal

     ©1993 ECS LEARNING SYSTEMS, INC., SAN ANTONIO, TEXAS   **11**

Pre-Unit Preparation

Part One

At least one month before this unit begins, the following needs to be accomplished:

1. Invite a speaker from the local Chamber of Commerce to acquaint the class with the services that are offered.

2. Gather materials for the learning center:

    Write letters requesting menus, lodging information, information about historical sites, etc.

    Ask the students to bring anything from home that relates to the unit.

    Meet with the media specialist to select appropriate literature and audio-visual materials.

    Select books from the library/media resource center.

    Find examples of expense logs.

    Collect maps and road atlases.

    Gather software.

    Gather craft materials.

    Meet with the music teacher to select appropriate music and musical activities.

Part Two

During the week before the unit starts, students should interview their parents. They should ask them for advice on planning a cross-country car trip. Students should prepare questions ahead of time, take notes during the interview, and be prepared to share this information during class discussion.

Letter to Parents

Dear Parent(s),

The children in my class are about to start a unit called "Travel Budget." In this unit, they will take an imaginary vacation using skills they have learned in math, social studies, health, art, reading, and language arts.

The children will be given certain guidelines to follow. Ask your child to share these guidelines with you. Part of the unit will include research to be used in an oral presentation which will be due on _____. You may want to take your child to the library to gather materials.

I know the children will benefit academically. They also will benefit socially through group participation and cooperative planning.

I'm looking forward to working with the class as they "travel" to new and exciting places.

If you have any questions, please feel free to contact me.

_____
Teacher's signature

_____
School phone number

Weekly
Schedules

Week 1

MONDAY

Introduction of unit—discuss cross-country car trips and the advice the students received from parents.

> Do "Vocabulary Knowledge Rating" from unit.
> Explain how the unit will work:
>> expectations
>> parameters
>> goals
>> packet
>> learning center

> Fill out "All About My Trip—Part One."
> Allow time for students to get into groups of three.

TUESDAY

> Fill out "Estimations" sheet.
> Complete "Places to Visit" sheet.
> Give lesson on the expense log. Use "Family Expense
> Record" sheet. Students must create their own log due on Trip Day 1.

WEDNESDAY

> Introduce library research.
> Present lesson on distance scales, map reading, and use of road maps.

THURSDAY

Present lesson relating United States history to the trip destinations.
Present lesson reviewing rounding, averaging, and ratios.

FRIDAY

Trip Day 1 and 2
Introduce students to using the learning center.
Ongoing activities:
Plot daily progress on road map.
Fill out packet sheets: "Fuel Sheet," "Lodging Record,"
"Food Budget," "Thermometer of Progress."
Bring expense log up to date.
Do library research.
Participate in learning center activities.

Week 2

MONDAY

Trip Day 3
Complete travel journal entry for days 1-3.
Ongoing activities:
Plot daily progress on road map.
Fill out packet sheets: "Fuel Sheet," "Lodging Record," "Food Budget," "Thermometer of Progress."
Bring expense log up to date.
Do library research.
Participate in learning center activities.

TUESDAY

Trip Day 4
Ongoing activities:
Plot daily progress on road map.
Fill out packet sheets: "Fuel Sheet," "Lodging Record," "Food Budget," "Thermometer of Progress."
Bring expense log up to date.
Do library research.
Participate in learning center activities.

WEDNESDAY

Trip Day 5
Ongoing activities:
Plot daily progress on road map.
Fill out packet sheets: "Fuel Sheet," "Lodging Record," "Food Budget," "Thermometer of Progress."
Bring expense log up to date.
Do library research.
Participate in learning center activities.
Optional activity:
Complete a postcard.

 ©1993 ECS LEARNING SYSTEMS, INC., SAN ANTONIO, TEXAS

THURSDAY

Trip Day 6
Ongoing activities:
Plot daily progress on road map.
Fill out packet sheets: "Fuel Sheet," "Lodging Record," "Food Budget," "Thermometer of Progress."
Bring expense log up to date.
Do library research.
Participate in learning center activities.

FRIDAY

Trip Day 7 and 8
Complete travel journal entry for days 4-7.
Ongoing activities:
Plot daily progress on road map.
Fill out packet sheets: "Fuel Sheet," "Lodging Record," "Food Budget," "Thermometer of Progress."
Bring expense log up to date.
Do library research.
Participate in learning center activities.

©1993 ECS LEARNING SYSTEMS, INC., SAN ANTONIO, TEXAS   **19**

Week 3

MONDAY

Trip Day 9
  Ongoing activities:
    Plot daily progress on road map.
    Fill out packet sheets: "Fuel Sheet," "Lodging Record," "Food Budget," "Thermometer of Progress."
    Bring expense log up to date.
    Do library research.
    Participate in learning center activities.
  Optional activity:
    Complete a postcard.

TUESDAY

Trip Day 10
  Complete travel journal entry for days 8-10.
  Ongoing activities:
    Plot daily progress on road map.
    Fill out packet sheets: "Fuel Sheet," "Lodging Record," "Food Budget," "Thermometer of Progress."
    Bring expense log up to date.
    Do library research.
    Participate in learning center activities.

WEDNESDAY

Trip Day 11
  Ongoing activities:
    Plot daily progress on road map.
    Fill out packet sheets: "Fuel Sheet," "Lodging Record," "Food Budget," "Thermometer of Progress."
    Bring expense log up to date.
    Do library research.
    Participate in learning center activities.

THURSDAY

Trip Day 12
> Begin planning oral presentations and visuals.
> Ongoing activities:
>> Plot daily progress on road map.
>> Fill out packet sheets: "Fuel Sheet," "Lodging Record," "Food Budget," "Thermometer of Progress."
>> Bring expense log up to date.
>> Do library research.
>> Participate in learning center activities.
> Optional activity:
>> Complete a postcard.
> Complete library research. Notecards due on Friday.

FRIDAY

Trip Day 13 and 14
> Complete packet sheets, road map, and expense log. Due Tuesday.
> Complete travel journal entry, days 11-14.
> Begin organizing notecards for oral presentation.

  ©1993 ECS LEARNING SYSTEMS, INC., SAN ANTONIO, TEXAS

Week 4

MONDAY

Present lesson on graphing. Use "Fun with Graphs." Graphs on daily
 mileage or daily expenses are due Tuesday.
Review "Thermometer of Progress" and the assignments that are due
 Tuesday.
Provide time to work on assignments due Tuesday.
Schedule oral presentations.

TUESDAY

Collect all assignments.
Complete "All About My Trip—Part Two."
Work on oral presentations.

WEDNESDAY

Oral presentations

THURSDAY

Oral presentations

FRIDAY

Revisit "Vocabulary Knowledge Rating" sheet filled out at the
 beginning of the unit.
Complete student self-evaluations.

Student
Packet

Vocabulary Knowledge Rating

Directions:

1. Find a partner.

2. Look at the first word on the list.

3. Decide if you can tell what the word means. If you can, put a check mark in the "Can Define" column.

4. If you cannot define the word, but have seen or heard it, put a check mark in the "Have Seen or Heard" column.

5. If you cannot define the word, and you have never seen or heard it before, put a check mark in the "Don't Know" column.

6. Continue marking the rest of the words in the same way.

7. Keep this sheet in a safe place until the end of the unit.

8. At the end of the unit, go back and see if you know more words than you did before.

 ©1993 ECS LEARNING SYSTEMS, INC., SAN ANTONIO, TEXAS

Vocabulary Knowledge Rating

		Can Define	Have Seen or Heard	Don't Know
1.	parameters	☐	☐	☐
2.	fuel	☐	☐	☐
3.	lodging	☐	☐	☐
4.	mpg	☐	☐	☐
5.	budget	☐	☐	☐
6.	route	☐	☐	☐
7.	distance scale	☐	☐	☐
8.	estimate	☐	☐	☐
9.	expense log	☐	☐	☐
10.	brochures	☐	☐	☐
11.	pamphlets	☐	☐	☐
12.	fliers	☐	☐	☐
13.	historical site	☐	☐	☐
14.	transportation	☐	☐	☐
15.	admission fee	☐	☐	☐
16.	mode of travel	☐	☐	☐
17.	museum	☐	☐	☐
18.	battlefield	☐	☐	☐
19.	odometer	☐	☐	☐
20.	travelogue	☐	☐	☐
21.	realia	☐	☐	☐

 ©1993 ECS LEARNING SYSTEMS, INC., SAN ANTONIO, TEXAS

Parameters

You are going on a vacation. You will be visiting some of the areas that we have covered in social studies. However, this trip is not free so you can only spend the amount of money in your budget. There will be certain places you need to visit and certain activities you will have to complete. Your goal is to visit the required places and do the required activities within the guidelines below.

1. Number of people who will go on the trip = 4
   (you, two travel buddies, and an adult member of your family who can drive the car)

2. Number of days = 14
   Leave from your home town on day 1 and return home on day 14.

3. Speed limit = 55 mph

4. Mileage limits per day = 400 miles maximum

5. Mode of travel = automobile
   Choose one of the following. You will need to find the mpg for the car you select.

   > Ford Escort
   > Chevy Suburban
   > Plymouth Voyager

6. Food—You must eat at least two meals per day and record your menu and prices.

 ©1993 ECS LEARNING SYSTEMS, INC., SAN ANTONIO, TEXAS

7. Cost of gasoline (regular unleaded) = $1.19 per gallon.

8. Lodging—Choose from the list below. You must stay at one of the following each night. You can mix and match. You don't have to stay at the same type of place every night.

      campgrounds
      motels/hotels
      relatives (maximum stay of two nights only)

9. Budget = $3,000.00

10. Grouping—Work with your travel buddies. When filling out the activity sheets, everyone in the group must agree to what is being filled out.

11. Places to visit—You must visit each of the following:

      one state/national park
      one battlefield
      two historical places
      one geographical location
      two museums
      one optional location

All About My Trip

Directions:

1. Choose two travel buddies. Together you will do some of the activities. Other activities, such as your travel journal, you will do by yourself.

2. With your travel buddies, make up a family to take this trip.

3. Fill out Part One, #1, "We are going."

4. Record the car you choose and its miles per gallon for # 2, "Transportation."

5. For Part One, #3, "Starting mileage," record the odometer reading from a parent's car—either yours or one of your travel buddies'.

6. On Tuesday of week four, fill out all of Part Two.

 ©1993 ECS LEARNING SYSTEMS, INC., SAN ANTONIO, TEXAS

All About My Trip
Part One

1. We are going

Name	Relationship	Age

2. Transportation

    Car _____

    Mpg _____

3. Starting mileage   ____ ____ ____ , ____ ____ ____ . ____

    (Get the odometer reading off a parent's car.)

       ©1993 ECS LEARNING SYSTEMS, INC., SAN ANTONIO, TEXAS

Part Two

1. Average distance traveled per day _____

2. Average cost per day for food _____

3. Visited _____ State/National Park
                 (name)

4. Admission/parking for 4 $ _____

Estimations

Estimate and Record

1. How much do you think you will spend for:

   Food? _____

   Lodging? _____

   Fuel? _____

   Total _____

2. What is the distance from:

   Home to destination? _____

3. How many times will you need to stop for fuel? _____

   ©1993 ECS LEARNING SYSTEMS, INC., SAN ANTONIO, TEXAS

Places to Visit

Directions:

Using your maps and travel brochures, choose a place to visit from each category. As you visit each location, fill out the name and state. After you have visited the required number of places in each category, place a check mark in the box for that category.

☐ **State/National Park**

_____

Name and State

☐ **Battlefield**

_____

Name and State

☐ **Important Historical Places** (At least two different states)

_____

Name and State

_____

Name and State

☐ **Geographical Location** (Example—ocean, mountain, etc.)

_____

Name and State

☐ **Museums** (Pick two)

_____

Name and State

_____

Name and State

Optional (Pick one)

☐ Visit Relatives

☐ Resorts

☐ "Tourist Traps"

☐ Zoos

☐ Amusement/Theme Parks

☐ _____ Other   (Something not on this list that
you found in research)

     ©1993 ECS LEARNING SYSTEMS, INC., SAN ANTONIO, TEXAS

Family Expense Record

Directions:

Here are some entries from the expense logs of families who have taken this trip. Calculate the amount of money each family spent by using the averages below:

$34.99 per night for lodging
$27.58 per day for fuel
$62.41 per day for meals

Family	Days on the Road	Total Spent
Taylor	7	$
Malat	4	$
Dorson	8	$
Heinz	5	$
Calas	10	$
King	3	$
McCarty	11	$
Parkis	12	$
Garcia	9	$
Humphrey	13	$
Meinike	15	$
Gualano	7	$
Saisi	14	$
Feinstein	5	$
Clark	8	$

 ©1993 ECS LEARNING SYSTEMS, INC., SAN ANTONIO, TEXAS

The Learning Center

Things that you will find in the learning center are as follows:

1. Menus received in answer to student letters (examples could include Denny's, McDonalds, Taco Bell, a pizza parlor, a Chinese restaurant, a favorite restaurant)

2. Pamphlets from campgrounds

3. Examples of expense logs

4. Brochures from national/state parks

5. Fliers from hotel/motel chains

6. Information from travel bureaus

7. Maps and road atlases

8. Selected literature

9. Filmstrips and cassettes

10. Video tapes

11. Photographs

12. Paintings

13. Materials to make "vanity" license plates

14. Materials to make salt and flour topographical maps

15. Record albums, cassettes, musical instruments, etc.

16. Calculators

     ©1993 ECS LEARNING SYSTEMS, INC., SAN ANTONIO, TEXAS

Fuel Sheet

Directions:

1. Record the odometer reading from a parent's car at the top of the sheet.

2. Each day of your imaginary trip, record your new odometer reading.

3. Next, figure out the distance you traveled, cost of gasoline, number of gallons used, and miles per gallon.

4. Record each of your answers on the "Fuel Sheet."

5. At the end of your trip, fill out the totals at the bottom of the page.

Fuel Sheet

Day	Odometer Reading	Distance Traveled	Cost of Gasoline	Number of Gallons	Miles per Gallon (Round to the nearest tenth)
Get reading from a parent's car					
1					
2					
3					
4					
5					
6					
7					
8					
9					
10					
11					
12					
13					
14					
Total	Final Odometer Reading	Distance Traveled	Cost of Gasoline	Number of Gallons	

©1993 ECS LEARNING SYSTEMS, INC., SAN ANTONIO, TEXAS

Lodging Record

Directions:

1. Keep in mind that you can choose from hotels, motels, and campgrounds. You are also allowed no more than two nights at a relative's house.

2. For each day, decide which type of lodging you stayed at, and based on the brochures that you received, record the cost for four people.

3. At the end of the trip, add up the total cost and record it.

 ©1993 ECS LEARNING SYSTEMS, INC., SAN ANTONIO, TEXAS

Lodging Record

Day	Where You Slept	Cost
1		
2		
3		
4		
5		
6		
7		
8		
9		
10		
11		
12		
13		
14		
	Total	

©1993 ECS LEARNING SYSTEMS, INC., SAN ANTONIO, TEXAS

Food Budget

Directions:

1. You and your travel buddies will need one food budget sheet for each day of your trip (Total—14).

2. For each day of your trip, complete the menu sheet and find your total daily budget. Complete the food budget sheet as follows:

   A. For each meal, record what each person ate and the cost of each meal.

   B. Calculate the total cost of each meal for all four people.

   C. Calculate your total daily food budget each day.

Food Budget

Plan your menu—Day #_____

	Meal 1	Cost	Meal 2	Cost	Meal 3	Cost	Snacks	Cost
Person 1								
Person 2								
Person 3								
Person 4								
	Total		Total		Total		Total	

Total Daily Food Budget _____

 ©1993 ECS LEARNING SYSTEMS, INC., SAN ANTONIO, TEXAS

Thermometer of Progress

Directions:

Starting at the bottom of the thermometer, shade in each section as you finish it.

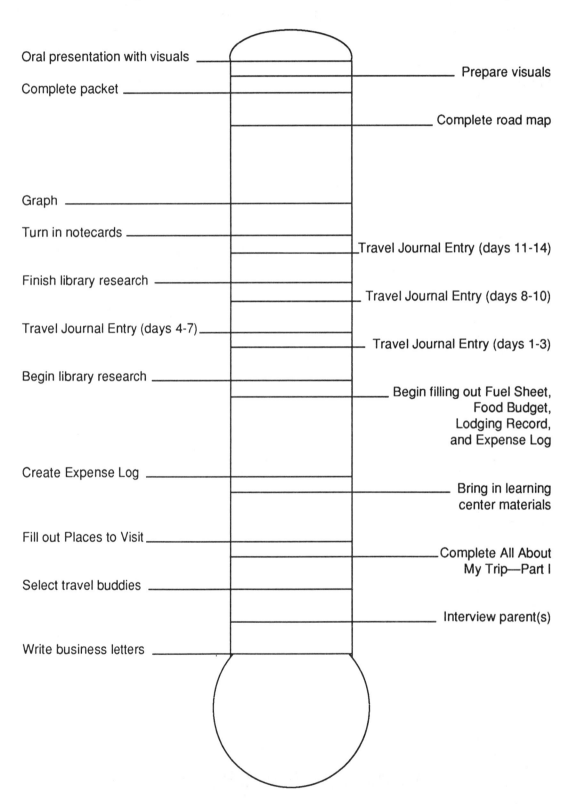

Oral presentation with visuals

Prepare visuals

Complete packet

Complete road map

Graph

Turn in notecards

Travel Journal Entry (days 11-14)

Finish library research

Travel Journal Entry (days 8-10)

Travel Journal Entry (days 4-7)

Travel Journal Entry (days 1-3)

Begin library research

Begin filling out Fuel Sheet, Food Budget, Lodging Record, and Expense Log

Create Expense Log

Bring in learning center materials

Fill out Places to Visit

Complete All About My Trip—Part I

Select travel buddies

Interview parent(s)

Write business letters

Travel Journal Entries

Pretend you are really on this trip. Of course, you will have to use your imagination. Try to figure out answers to some of the following questions:

What are you seeing along the way?
What places have you visited?
What was the best/worst experience you had?
How is the budget working out?
Have you had any car trouble?
Other problems? Illness? Lost luggage?
Did some of the historical sites meet your expectations?

You can write about these things in your travel journal. You must write journal entries at the end of Trip Day 3, 7, 10, and 14. Don't just list what is happening. Write about your *response* to it. What are you *thinking* and *feeling*?

Make your own travel journal. It can be in any format you want. For example, you can use a spiral notebook or you can staple pages of stationery together. Just be sure to put the trip day number at the top of each page.

You have done many of the activities from this trip with your travel buddies. However, each person must compete his/her own travel journal.

          ©1993 ECS LEARNING SYSTEMS, INC., SAN ANTONIO, TEXAS

Oral Presentation

The purpose of your oral presentation is to share your expertise about ONE of the places that you visited.

1. Pick your favorite place from the first five categories of your "Places to Visit" sheet.

2. Do research to find out all you can about your choice. Use a variety of sources.

3. Tell all about the place you chose. Each person in the group must pick a different place.

4. To share your expertise with the class, choose one of the ways below or a teacher-approved alternative that is not on the list.

> oral report to classmates
>
> oral report to a younger group of students
>
> a play
>
> historical re-enactment
>
> time line
>
> puppet show
>
> travelogue on audio or video cassette
>
> commercial
>
> filmstrip made and narrated by you

 ©1993 ECS LEARNING SYSTEMS, INC., SAN ANTONIO, TEXAS

5. Include a visual aid with your presentation.

poster

postcards

maps

diorama

photographs, slides

travel brochure written by you

realia—example: copy of the Declaration of Independence

 ©1993 ECS LEARNING SYSTEMS, INC., SAN ANTONIO, TEXAS

Postcards

Directions:

At the end of trip days 5, 9, and 12, you and your travel buddies may choose to send postcards to the folks back home.

There are two sides to each postcard. On the front, draw and color a picture representing one of the areas you have visited. On the back, there are many things you need to do:

1. In the upper left corner, write a brief description of the picture drawn on the front.

2. Write your message on the left side of the postcard, under the description.

3. Design and color a stamp.

4. Address the postcard.

Cut out the front and back of the postcard and glue them together. You may want to use all three postcards as part of your visuals for your oral presentation.

Postcards

Front of Postcard

Back of Postcard

To: _____

_____

_____

_____

Fun with Graphs

When you gather and organize information dealing with numbers, you are using statistics. This is the science of collecting numerical data. By using graphs, you are able to show your statistics in a useful and clear way. Graphs help others understand your information through visual comparison.

You can find out more about yourself, your lifestyle, and the world around you through the use of simple mathematics.

There are four main types of graphs:

> Line graph
> Pie graph
> Bar graph
> Pictograph

The graph you use will depend upon what information you would like to present.

The **line graph** is good for continuous information and showing changes through time.

Do you think students miss school more on one day than any other day of the week? Which day do you think it would be? Attendance was taken for one school year in a fourth-grade class. Out of thirty-five students, they missed a total of forty-two days of school. Students were absent sixteen times on Mondays, three times on Tuesdays, two times on Wednesdays, six times on Thursdays, and fifteen times on Fridays.

Explaining the information is okay, but showing the results in the form of a line graph helps us to see the results.

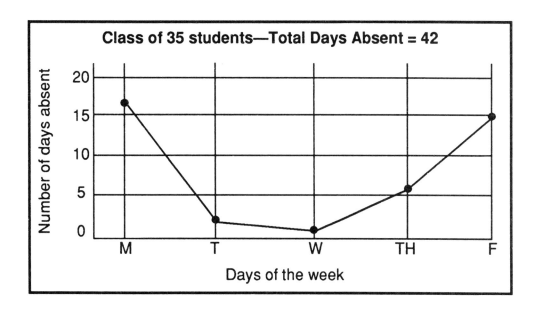

Things needed to make a line graph:

  a pencil
  ruler
  graph paper
  information or data

 ©1993 ECS LEARNING SYSTEMS, INC., SAN ANTONIO, TEXAS

Line graph patterns

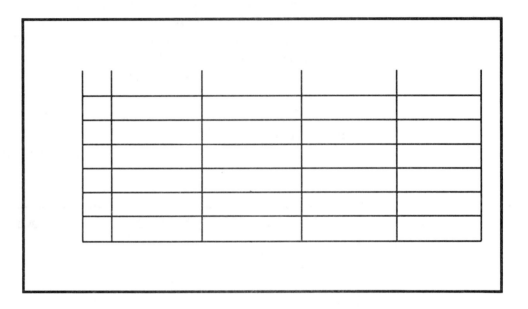

The **pie graph** gets its name because it looks like a pie divided into pieces. A pie graph shows how the whole is divided. It is good for showing percentages or parts of the whole.

Suppose you like to roller skate on Friday evenings. You are trying to convince a friend how much fun it would be if he or she came along. The following pie chart shows how many boys, girls, and adults are usually at the skating rink on a Friday evening.

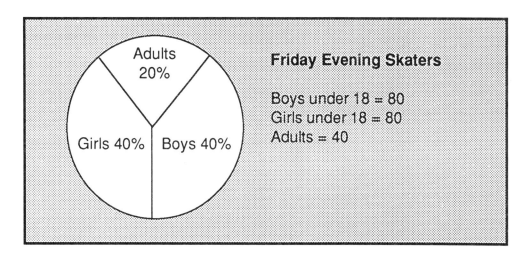

A pie graph could also show how you spend your time on a typical Saturday.

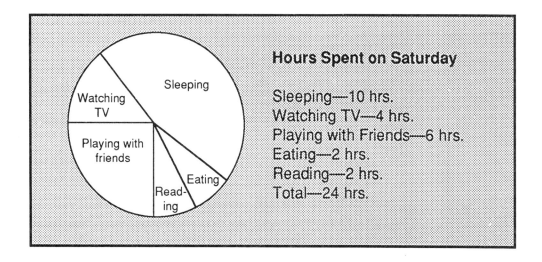

     ©1993 ECS LEARNING SYSTEMS, INC., SAN ANTONIO, TEXAS

Pie graph patterns

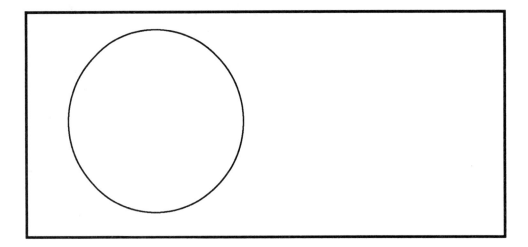

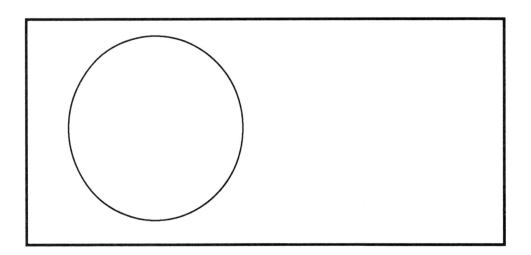

The **bar graph** is helpful when you are making simple comparisons and want someone to see your data at a glance. What kind of weather do you most enjoy? The following bar graph shows four cities in the United States with their average annual temperature. See, at a glance, where you might live most comfortably.

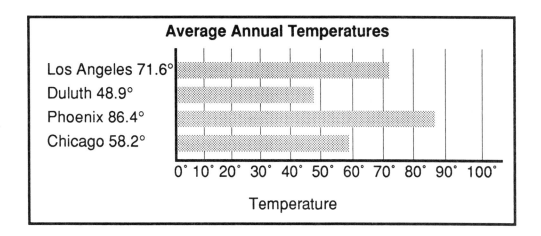

What causes most accidental deaths in the United States? In 1983, 44,600 people died from motor vehicle accidents. Three thousand people died from poisoning. This comparison could be shown using a bar graph and the information would be much clearer. When a graph line stops halfway between two numbers, for example between 40,000 and 50,000, your number is about halfway between those two figures, or in this case, 45,000.

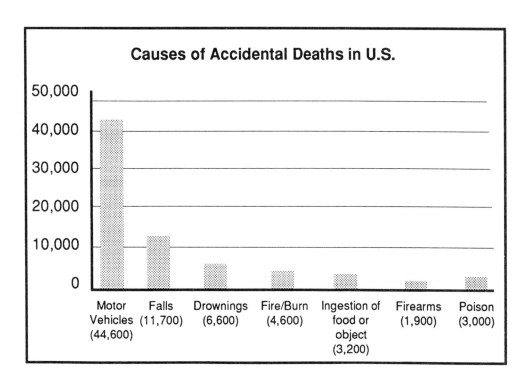

   ©1993 ECS LEARNING SYSTEMS, INC., SAN ANTONIO, TEXAS

Bar graph patterns

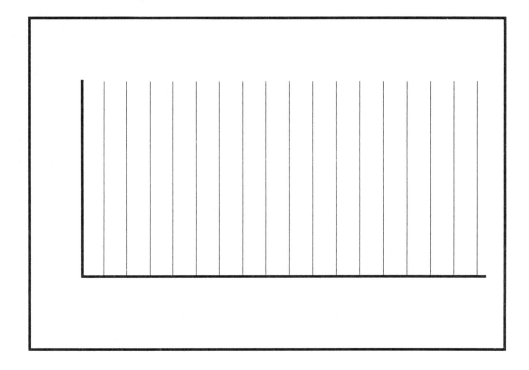

 ©1993 ECS LEARNING SYSTEMS, INC., SAN ANTONIO, TEXAS

The **pictograph** uses pictures instead of bars. For example, if you were talking about time, you might use clocks as symbols in your graph. When the subject is money, the dollar bill sign could be drawn.

Try making a pictograph of how much time it takes you to get home from school. You could time yourself using four different modes of transportation—walking, school bus, bicycling, or car.

Travel Time—School to Home

Walking	🕐 🕐 🕐 🕐 🕐
Bus	🕐 🕐
Bike	🕐 🕐 🕐
Car	🕐 🕐 = five minutes

You might earn money by doing certain chores. But which chores will earn you the most money in the shortest amount of time? A pictograph can help you *see* the answer.

Making Money Chores (dollars earned per hour)

Shoveling snow	$ $ $ $ $
Babysitting	$ $ $
Mowing Lawns	$ $ $ $
Raking Leaves	$ $ $
	$ = one dollar

Pictograph patterns

Think of something that interested you during your trip. Gather facts and decide what type of graph would be most useful to show your information. How much did you spend for food? lodging? fuel? How many days did you spend at campgrounds? at motels/hotels? with relatives? Why not try a pie graph showing how you spent a typical day on your trip?

Use your imagination when designing your graph. It could be simple and direct or have lots of color and unique style. The purpose is to convey a message, so be sure your graphs are titled and clearly labeled. You may find graphs a nice supplement to your homework assignments.

 ©1993 ECS LEARNING SYSTEMS, INC., SAN ANTONIO, TEXAS

Evaluation

Evaluation

This section contains a variety of assessment tools. They can be used along with the unit assignments to evaluate student progress.

The "Rating Scale—Oral Presentation" sheet should be filled out by the teacher after students give their oral reports. The rest of the evaluations should be completed at the end of the unit.

Rating Scale—Oral Presentation

This sheet is to be completed by the teacher after students give their oral reports. The scale at the top of the sheet is to be used to rate each item.

Student Self-Evaluation Checklist

Each student should consider the statements on the checklist and put a check mark in the appropriate column.

Student Self-Evaluation Essay Questions

Each student should answer all the questions in complete sentences.

We Cooperated!

Each group of travel buddies works together to complete this evaluation.

Interdisciplinary Teacher Self-Evaluation

At the end of the unit, the teacher decides which goals were implemented and which ones need to be considered for the next unit.

Along with these assessment tools, teachers can also evaluate the unit by their students' active participation and enthusiasm.

Rating Scale
Oral Presentation

4- Outstanding

3- Above Average

2- Good

1- Needs Improvement

Content

The topic is well-researched. _____

There are a variety of resources used. _____

The report stays on the topic. _____

The report is well-organized. _____

The report is well-prepared. _____

An introduction and conclusion are included. _____

The information given is accurate. _____

Presentation

The student:

uses audio/visual aids

_____

projects voice

_____

shows enthusiasm and interest in the topic

_____

uses appropriate gestures and body movements
while speaking

_____

maintains eye contact

_____

uses good intonation

_____

avoids using interrupters (such as uh, and...)

_____

        ©1993 ECS LEARNING SYSTEMS, INC., SAN ANTONIO, TEXAS

Student Self-Evaluation
Checklist

	Most of the time	Sometimes	Seldom
I was a good listener during oral presentations.	☐	☐	☐
I accurately used estimations.	☐	☐	☐
I am a better map reader now.	☐	☐	☐
My research skills have improved.	☐	☐	☐
I can write a business letter.	☐	☐	☐
I was able to stay within my budget.	☐	☐	☐
I ate nutritious meals.	☐	☐	☐
I feel good about my journal responses.	☐	☐	☐
I accurately filled out my fuel and food budget sheets.	☐	☐	☐
I am able to make and interpret graphs.	☐	☐	☐
I am more familiar with historical sites.	☐	☐	☐
My oral presentation was interesting and well-organized.	☐	☐	☐
The visual aid went well with my presentation.	☐	☐	☐
I made good use of the learning center.	☐	☐	☐

Student Self-Evaluation

Essay Questions

1. What could you have done to plan your trip better? Explain.

2. Look over your estimation sheet. Compare your estimations to your actual figures. How close are the two figures? Explain.

        ©1993 ECS LEARNING SYSTEMS, INC., SAN ANTONIO, TEXAS

3. What was your favorite part of this unit? Why?

4. What did you like least about this unit? Why?

5. How could this unit be improved for next year's class?

6. What advice would you give someone who is planning a trip?

  ©1993 ECS LEARNING SYSTEMS, INC., SAN ANTONIO, TEXAS

We Cooperated!

Team Members

A. _____

B. _____

C. _____

1. We distributed the jobs fairly.

	Yes	No
A.	☐	☐
B.	☐	☐
C.	☐	☐

2. Everyone contributed.

	Yes	No
A.	☐	☐
B.	☐	☐
C.	☐	☐

3. We got along well together.

	Yes	No
A.	☐	☐
B.	☐	☐
C.	☐	☐

4. We were able to solve problems
    that came up.

	Yes	No
A.	☐	☐
B.	☐	☐
C.	☐	☐

5. We remembered to use our quiet voices.

	Yes	No
A.	☐	☐
B.	☐	☐
C.	☐	☐

                    ©1993 ECS LEARNING SYSTEMS, INC., SAN ANTONIO, TEXAS

6. Some things we did well are

_____

_____

_____

_____

_____

_____

_____

_____

_____

_____

_____

7.   Some things we can do better next time are

_____

_____

_____

_____

_____

_____

_____

_____

_____

_____

_____

_____

WE GOT THE JOB DONE!

©1993 ECS LEARNING SYSTEMS, INC., SAN ANTONIO, TEXAS

Teacher Self-Evaluation

This form may be used at the completion of an interdisciplinary unit.

	Implemented	Goal for next unit
Applications		
I provided opportunities for the students to transfer what they learned in the classroom to real-life situations.	_____	_____
I successfully integrated several areas of the curriculum.	_____	_____
I increased the students' abilities to interpret data.	_____	_____
I collaborated with others in preparing this unit.	_____	_____
I allowed children to learn in a holistic manner.	_____	_____
I met specific curriculum objectives.	_____	_____
I used flexible scheduling.	_____	_____
I assessed student progress.	_____	_____

	Implemented	Goal for next unit

Communication

I conferred on a regular basis with each student.	_____	_____
I encouraged the use of good listening skills.	_____	_____
I allowed students to share their experiences.	_____	_____
I provided opportunities for public speaking.	_____	_____
I made sure students had many opportunities to write for a purpose.	_____	_____
I reported student progress to parents.	_____	_____
I allowed students to share what they had learned.	_____	_____

Teaching Strategies

I included cooperative learning strategies.	_____	_____
I remembered to use "wait time."	_____	_____
I modeled research-based reading strategies.	_____	_____
I encouraged students to use good vocabulary skills.	_____	_____
I selected developmentally appropriate activities.	_____	_____
I combined good teaching techniques with learning theories.	_____	_____
I gave students practice in problem solving.	_____	_____
I enabled students to practice critical thinking skills.	_____	_____
I helped students improve their reading skills.	_____	_____

 ©1993 ECS LEARNING SYSTEMS, INC., SAN ANTONIO, TEXAS

	Implemented	Goal for next unit

Resources/Research

I furnished materials at different levels of difficulty. _____ _____

I expanded my own professional growth. _____ _____

I gathered a variety of resources. _____ _____

Environment

I established a positive reading environment. _____ _____

I accommodated the needs and interests of individual students. _____ _____

I empowered students to help make decisions. _____ _____

I encouraged students to take risks. _____ _____

I offered encouragement and positive feedback. _____ _____

I gave students choices. _____ _____

Travel Notes

_____

_____

_____

_____

_____

_____

_____

_____

_____

_____

_____

_____

_____

 ©1993 ECS LEARNING SYSTEMS, INC., SAN ANTONIO, TEXAS

Travel Notes

_____

_____

_____

_____

_____

_____

_____

_____

_____

_____

_____

_____

_____

Travel Notes

_____

_____

_____

_____

_____

_____

_____

_____

_____

_____

_____

_____

About the Authors

Marian Diana Costello

Marian Diana Costello graduated from Concordia University with a master's degree in curriculum and instruction. Ms. Costello was a sixth-grade language arts teacher in Chicago, Illinois, taught remedial reading in North Carolina, and is currently preschool coordinator for the Arlington Heights Park District in Illinois. She is a free-lance writer who has published both fiction and nonfiction in various national publications and has presented writing and publishing seminars.

Marian and Jim Costello have been married for 19 years and have two daughters, Jaclyn and Jennifer.

Carol Rito McGrath

Carol Rito McGrath has been a teacher in the Des Plaines Elementary Schools for the past twenty-five years. She holds a master's degree in curriculum and instruction. She is a firm believer in the writing workshop approach to teaching students to write and has had a writing workshop in her classroom since 1984. Ms. McGrath is a free-lance writer who is a regular contributor to *Writing Teacher*™ magazine, where she is on the editorial advisory panel. She has taught graduate level classes for teachers on writing across the curriculum. She has also given numerous inservice presentations on teaching writing.

Ms. McGrath lives in Arlington Heights, Illinois, with her husband Pete. They have one son, Matt, and three grandchildren.

Dagmar Kosack Rutzen

Dagmar Kosack Rutzen holds a Bachelor of Science degree and a Master of Arts in the area of curriculum and instruction. Ms. Rutzen was educated in Germany, France, and the United States. Her teaching duties have ranged all the way from preschool to college, including work with the physically and mentally handicapped. Currently she teaches math and science with a heavy hands-on approach at the junior high level in Des Plaines, Illinois.

This approach has led students through a local archaeological program in the field, as well as in the classroom. Historical re-enactments have brought to life the town's history and how the students fit into their environment. A unique outdoor education program also gives the students a chance to experience activities that they may never encounter in the regular classroom. By actively engaging students in a variety of activities, Ms. Rutzen is trying to provide many different learning opportunities for her students.